A Sportin...
with *2Kplus*

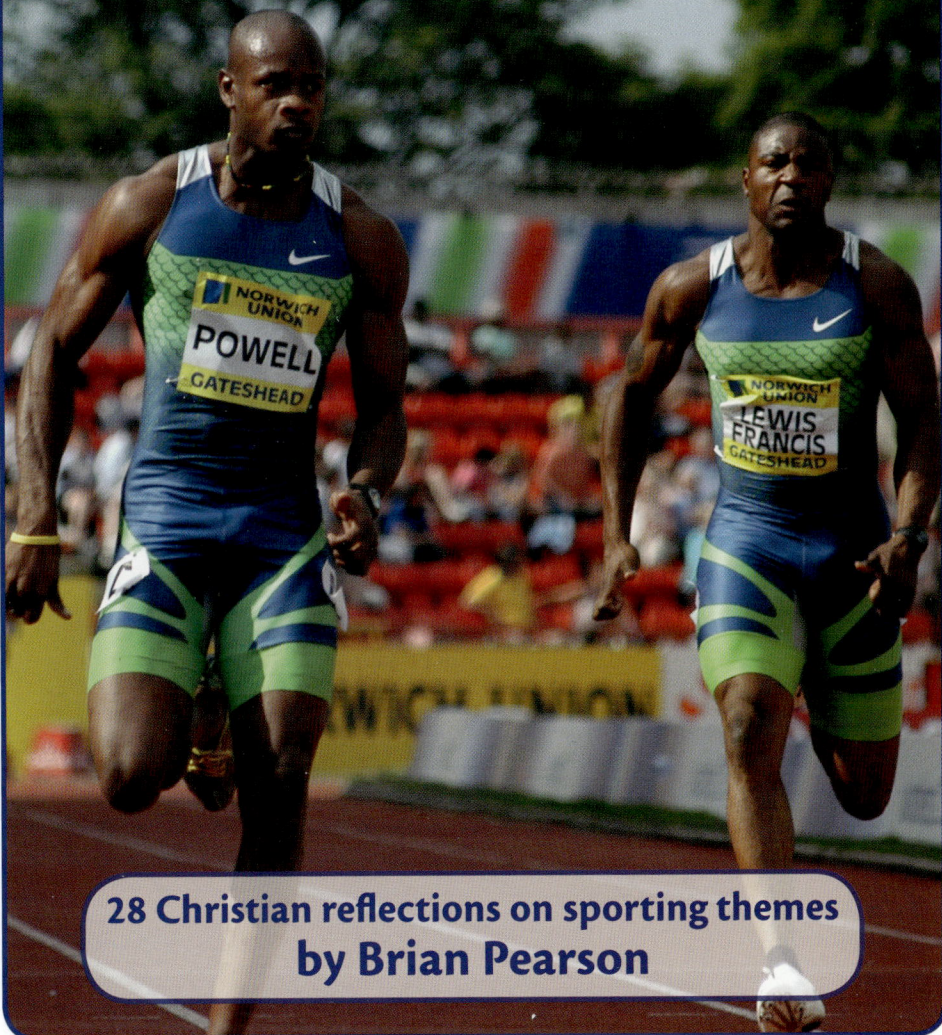

POWELL
GATESHEAD

LEWIS FRANCIS
GATESHEAD

**28 Christian reflections on sporting themes
by Brian Pearson**

Wild Duck Productions

Produced by 2K Plus International Sports Media

2K Plus International Sports Media is a company limited by guarantee number 4286195
and a registered charity number 1091941

Published in 2012 by Wild Duck Productions
Telephone: 0871 218 2183
Website: www.wildduckproductions.com

ISBN 978-0-9556491-1-0

British Library Cataloguing in Publication Data
A catalogue record for this book is available from the British Library

PHOTO CREDITS: Adrian Barnard, Danny Rice, Norman Brierley, Solomon Izang Ashoms,
Marcos Falcao, Martin Bateman (Enigma-Sports), Stuart Weir, Tara Olonga. Bigstockphoto.com library:
page 10 – arenacreative/Bigstock.com; page 14 – wallbanger/Bigstock.com; page 18 – Zevark/Bigstock.com;
page 22 – Spanishalex/Bigstock.com; page 28 – flippo/Bigstock.com; page 44 – keithpix/Bigstock.com;
page 50 – Rinderart/Bigstock.com; page 54 – Lance Bellers/Bigstock.com; page 58 – Photosani/Bigstock.com;
page 61 (Mandela) ivanerios/Bigstock.com; Check the manual boxes – IngridHS/Bigstock.com

Designed by Christopher Lawther, Worthing, West Sussex
thelawthers@ntlworld.com

Printed by Kenads, Goring-by-Sea, West Sussex
www.kenadsprinters.co.uk

2K plus

INTERNATIONAL SPORTS MEDIA

**Your support in giving and prayer is vital as we seek
to introduce sports fans to Jesus and help those
who already follow Jesus to grow in their faith.**

There are several ways you can get involved and help:

1 Keep in touch and receive our regular newsletters

2 Receive our fortnightly email prayer bulletin

3 Organise a 2K Plus Quiz and Auction at your church

4 Send a donation. You may like to sponsor a Planet Sport programme
on one radio station for one week for just £7.25
or you can send a general donation to help us introduce
sports fans to Jesus and encourage existing
followers of Jesus in their faith.

If you would like to support 2K Plus International Sports Media
or would like further information we would love to hear from you.
You can contact us at the addresses below:

Email: office@2kplus.org.uk

Address: 2K Plus International Sports Media
Box 4436
Worthing
West Sussex   BN14 7WH

Telephone: 01903-217727

Websites: www.2kplus.org.uk
www.planetsport.tv

Facebook: www.facebook.com/planetsportmedia

Twitter: www.twitter.com/planetsporttv

Foreword

Rt Revd Mark Rylands, *Bishop of Shrewsbury*

Brian Pearson's writing is like his bowling – a lively pace, always on a length and with a cunning late swing that you have to watch carefully as a batsman. This intelligent and hopeful writer is passionate about sport and about Jesus Christ.

A Sporting Month with 2K Plus, with its engaging style and thought-provoking content, will grab your attention and make you think. Brian helps to draw us closer to the God who is passionate about this planet and all sports fans who live on it.

I am delighted to commend it.

+ Mark

2K *plus* International Sports Media exists for the sports fan. It aims to show that following Jesus Christ is relevant for the sports fan in the 21st century and that living according to Jesus' teaching offers the best lifestyle around.

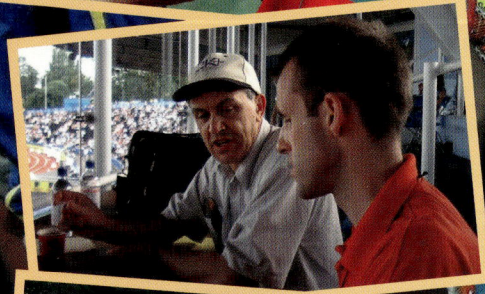

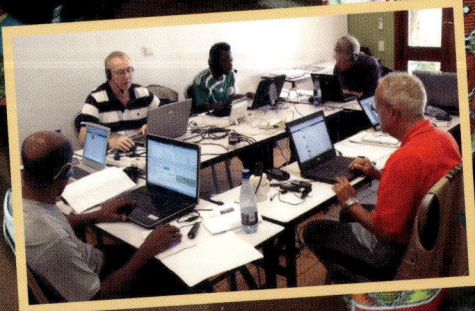

2Kplus
INTERNATIONAL SPORTS MEDIA

About the author

BRIAN PEARSON'S passion for and participation in sport spans over 50 years. A football referee for 22 years and currently an ECB umpire and coach and enthusiastic player, he continues to relish involvement in sport. He has officiated at Football League grounds and plays cricket for Somerset Over 60s.

He has toured Zimbabwe as a member of a Christians in Sport cricket squad and has also played in Barbados and South Africa with Warwickshire Over 50s. Memorable moments? Hitting a six at Newlands, the picturesque international ground at the foot of Table Mountain and claiming the wickets of two county cricketers.

Brian has written for the Christian press and is the author of books on church management. He has written and presented several series of *Thoughts* for television and wrote and performed

Brian (above, right), and below effortlessly caressing another ball to the boundary

Belief Encounters, a set of dramatic portrayals of new testament characters (http://www.beliefencounters.com/).

Brian was ordained as a Church of England minister in 1979 and has served as Archbishop George Carey's Officer for Mission and Evangelism. He has worked in parishes in South London, Sussex, Warwickshire and Somerset. Brian holds a first degree in Computer Science, and Masters degrees in Business Systems Design and in Applied Theology. He is married to Althea, a Consultant Counselling Psychologist and they have two adult sons.

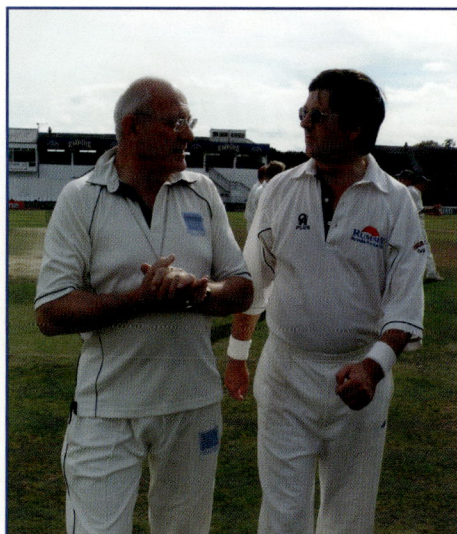

Heading for the finishing line

T makes no difference how long a race is, there has to be a last lap or a final furlong or the home stretch. Everything that goes before is important; it is like the investment that comes before actually cashing in and reaping the benefits.

Throughout our lives we are shaping, modifying and implementing a game plan. Most of the time we are likely to be quite unaware of it but it is inevitable that our preparations, our decisions and our character will play a part in just how we face up to each phase of the journey from the start to the finish.

But here is something odd, well unique, actually. Our journey in life, which we might think of as a race with an inevitable end, holds an element of mystery. And the mystery is: where and when it ends. We know there will be an end but we do not know the time, nor the place, nor the circumstances of its happening.

Is that unnerving? Well, for some it is and their motto is: live each day as if it were your last! But there is a danger in that as it may encourage a self-centred approach to all that we do. There are other perspectives we can adopt which no less recognise that an end will come.

One way is to reject the game plan approach; play it by ear, try to adjust on the spur of the moment, do away with preparing or weighing up options. Most of us know someone who seems content to go with the flow through life but too often

Our journey in life ... holds an element of mystery

the uncertainty and lack of foresight create problems that make the journey of life overwhelming. Another way is to adopt a Christian perspective, living each day to the full while anticipating that, one day, the race will be over and, yes, also that the reward will be granted. But until that time the game plan will continue to unfold bit by bit.

As with any game plan we have to adjust our efforts and attitudes to meet the inevitable changes in the conditions we encounter. But those adjustments are not made randomly nor on a whim; they are prompted by a constant desire to prayerfully and carefully adapt to a different and better way of being.

Reaching the finish is assured, whenever that may be, but arriving knowing that we have achieved what was required of us, is as humbling as it is fulfilling.

Check the manual:

Hebrews 12:1-2

Tell it like it is

THE task of the coach can be a thankless one. Despite every effort, the rigorous training schedule, the attention to detail, the goading, the encouraging, the shared insights and wisdom, there comes that moment when all that is left to do is to watch. The player steps out onto the pitch or court, the athlete steps onto the track and has to perform.

Parents, along with coaches, have lived this experience thousands of times and they know it doesn't end with the stepping out. Afterwards, _something_ has to be said. In success, the actual words may be lost in celebration but something has to be said. If the result comes shrouded in disappointment, again, _something has to be said_.

Finding the right words to say is a part of life. What we say to one another reveals something of ourselves and even more about our relationships. And while there are times when it is right to be silent, to simply 'be', even the silence has to be broken and then both what is said and how it is said are so important.

Some of the important things we say come from the head such as when the coach has analysed the athlete's performance and passes on observations and technical advice. But usually the most important things we say come from the heart. These are weighted by

the feeling that drives them, the passion, the depth, perhaps even the need to release a burden.

There is a world of difference between saying what we think and saying what we believe and the Christian desire to let others know of our faith will be heart-driven as much as, if not more than, mind-driven. And, yes, I know, that is so much easier for me to write than for any of us to do.

So what can be said? Tell it as it is. There is no story more authentic to share than your own. It does not have to be glossy or dramatic let alone worthy of being made into a movie. Indeed, simple is profound. And yet simple can be amazing when it is the story of a life changed for ever.

The most effective words from the coach will be those which are sincere, honest, positive and well-intentioned. They will also be offered within a trusting relationship. Maybe that is a good basis for us when we are presented with an opportunity to share our faith. We may not all be eloquent, but we are who we have been made, and, if others are willing to listen, let's be ready to speak.

Check the manual:
Proverbs 24:26; Zechariah 8:16; Ephesians 4:15

How serious is that?

"**YOU** cannot be serious!" To do it justice, that utterance really needs to be spaced out, set in capitals and adorned with a few more exclamation marks. Let me try again: **YOU CAN NOT BE SERIOUS!!!!** That's more like it.

Whatever it was the charismatic tennis star, John McEnroe, wished to communicate with those words, it was probably not an understatement. His view could not have been made more clear. By comparison, so many utterances offered in the name of the Christian faith are cringingly wimpish. Words are arcane, phrases clichéd, sentences convoluted, paragraphs unintelligible. How sad that something so important becomes so obscured by the very words used to express it.

It was so, so refreshing to overhear a teenage girl who was being goaded about her refusal to participate in a questionable activity, say, with maximum eye contact, "Because I'm a Christian; you got a problem with that?" You cannot be serious? She was. And well done her, I say.

Of course that sort of confrontation may seem light years away from anything experienced by those who were witnesses to the great events of Jesus' life, death and resurrection. They had watched him, listened to him, quizzed him and, in turn, been bemused and confused by him. And yet when he had gone and his Spirit had swept them up and sorted them out, they were as in-yer-face as was McEnroe, with a little less of the attitude, and that teenage girl.

I have the impression of the apostle Paul being a crusty and crotchety sort – a possible model for a later McEnroe, perhaps. After all, he had been blasted into belief on the Damascus road, viewed with understandable suspicion by those he had previously been persecuting and then he embarked upon a series of journeys which were punctuated with beatings, imprisonment, a shipwreck and political as well as religious opposition. Not many good hair days for Paul in that lot.

But Paul never let go of his conviction that he had discovered the most serious thing in the whole of creation. While the authorities, the mockers, and the fearful were saying: You cannot be serious! Paul was ploughing, at times, a very lonely furrow which serves to underline just how serious were both he and his message.

So how seriously do you take it? Seriously enough to know what you believe? Good start. Seriously enough to examine what you believe? That's better. Seriously enough to share what you believe? That's crunch time, isn't it? And perhaps the really big crunch comes when someone says to you: YOU CAN NOT BE SERIOUS! And you can reply: MORE SERIOUS THAN YOU COULD EVER BELIEVE!

Check the manual:

Acts 9:1-19;
2 Corinthians 11:24-31

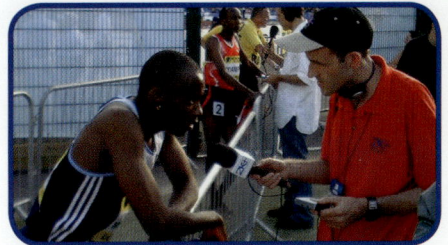

So what motivates you?

A track event in athletics can be over in a matter of seconds or maybe a few minutes. A marathon will take at least a couple of hours. What do they have in common; well, lots of things – probably starting with some decent footwear!

Actually I was thinking more about before the off, long before the off, in fact; weeks and months, maybe even years, before the moment when, hopefully, it will all come together. It is in that period, in the long hours and days of training and preparation that the foundation is laid for even beginning to believe that qualifying for, let alone competing at, the highest level is a possibility. Here, there is no place for the fair-weather athlete; no place for oversleeping and missing a gruelling two hours in the gym or

All who aspire to be the best can tell stories of sacrifice

pounding the streets while others dream on. For these dedicated souls, any dreaming has to be done when wide awake and while it hurts!

All who aspire to be the best can tell stories of sacrifice, of going through the

pain barrier one more time and yet they do it and would, quite truthfully, have it no other way. Something must motivate them, and motivate them far beyond what others would consider reasonable.

Perhaps even more than being motivated, these people seem to be compelled to press on, to keep raising the bar, to become increasingly focussed upon a single goal. They will not be distracted; they will not be deterred; they will not be less than best.

But there are other costs to count. As the intensity increases some athletes find themselves distanced from colleagues, friends and even family. "Is anything really that important?" they are asked. And it is a question to which the answer is blatantly obvious.

And what of us? We who will not, realistically, be among those eyeing the podium which honours those who attain their goals. Yet we do have goals, modest though they may seem by comparison. And yes, we can be motivated. Even if the physical excellence of star athletes is beyond us, we can experience a depth of motivation to live the best life there is.

What could possibly be that motivation? No surprises; it is love and a love that is within such easy reach of us all. It is an overwhelming love and an all embracing love and an unconditional love. It is the love of Christ which compels us; compels us to be the person God intended each of us to be.

And suppose we do respond; suppose we are motivated? Will it be pain free? Probably not. Will it make demands upon us? More than likely. Will it be worth it? Definitely.

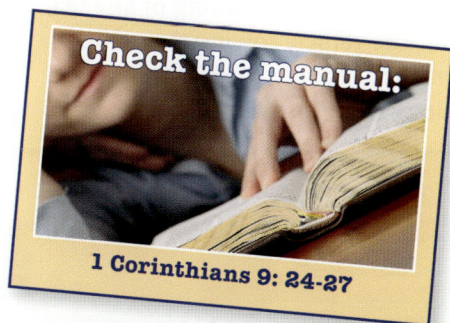

Check the manual:

1 Corinthians 9: 24-27

Disaster and despair transformed

HE arrived too late for the start of the match and so a substitute took his place. She had swum hundreds of lengths in preparation then, two days before the competition, twisted her ankle as she stepped off a bus. They had built a craft that would withstand the pounding of any sea, but the vehicle towing the trailer crashed, leaving the boat shattered along with their dreams.

No, these instances, and so many more you and I could add from our own experience, are not merely a matter of

... then come the "if only" thoughts which fuel not only regret but also guilt

"oh dear, what a shame, never mind" but are, for those directly involved,

totally devastating. All the investment, both physical and emotional, that had gone into the endeavour, had become worth nothing. These are situations which are irretrievable, and they are nothing short of gut-wrenchingly awful.

And if that were not bad enough, then come the "if only" thoughts which fuel not only regret but also guilt. This is not about a superficial disappointment, it is about a depth of disappointment and despair from which, at that moment, there is no glimpse of a way to recover or restore what has, it would seem, been snatched away.

And yet we also have many examples of what we call the human spirit fighting against this, of trying to turn defeat into victory, trying to transform despair into hope, trying to redefine loss as gain. To our logical minds this way of thinking may seem at best baffling and at worst futile. But whatever it is, it is a remarkably close impression of God's Holy Spirit which will not give in and which has turned apparent defeat into actual victory, has transformed utter despair into real hope and has even brought life from death.

For those followers of Christ who looked death in the face and felt no fear, it was the comfort and strength of this same Spirit that made it possible. For those who sacrificed everything for what they knew to be true, it was the Spirit which empowered them. And for us it is also the same Spirit who can lead us from the depths of despair to experience a contentment and fulfilment beyond our understanding.

I have yet to meet anyone who relishes disappointment but I know many who have come to face it with renewed confidence and hope by putting their faith in the power of the Holy Spirit. To do so requires at one and the same time a simple step and a bold step, indeed, a step of faith. But, as I once heard some-one say, "A little faith can go a long way."

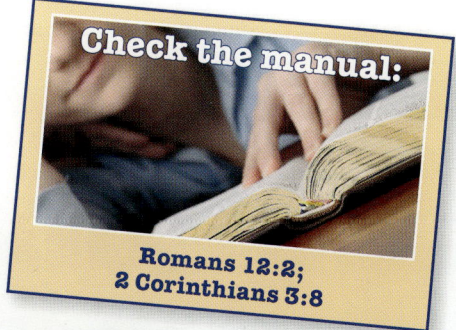

Check the manual:

Romans 12:2;
2 Corinthians 3:8

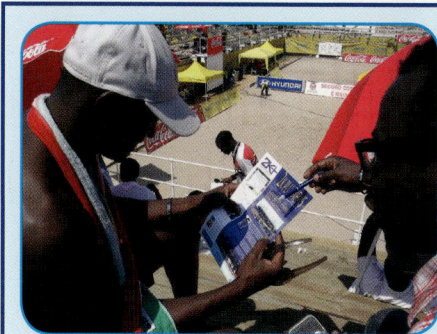

2K plus produces a regular newsletter featuring news, information, prayer points and interviews with Christian sportsmen and women. We would love to send this to you to keep in touch with the ministry.

To receive your copy contact Peter Ellis: office@2kplus.org.uk or telephone 01903-217727.

It's all over – or is it?

"**T**HEY think it's all over … It is now!" In 1966 BBC TV commentator Kenneth Wolstenholme uttered those words which he could never have believed would become immortalised.

But now for the almost unforgivable; I am going to add to those revered words: "They think it's all over … It is now!" with "And it was but it wasn't". Which, I admit, doesn't seem to make sense and therefore, you might think, was hardly worth my adding.

But I have to add those words, because without them we do not have the full story. With the blowing of the final whistle in that FIFA World Cup Final played at Wembley, the match was over, time to pack up and go home. It was finished.

But it wasn't; the debate about the validity of a disputed goal which turned the game in England's favour had hardly begun. Did the whole of the ball cross the whole of the line?

More than forty years on, with the aid of remarkable technology, the

controversy continues to be re-visited and re-examined; computer-simulation has been employed and the whole episode has even been the subject of serious, mathematical, academic papers. And in spite of all that, the conclusion is, well, inconclusive!

Two thousand years before that commentator was doing his job, it would not have been unreasonable for

... the bottom line is that each of us who is open to the truth, can find the truth

certain authority figures in the Middle East to be heard muttering, as nails were slammed through bare flesh into a wooden crossbeam "They think it's all over" and a few hours later as a body was carried away, to add, "It is now". But, as we know, it was … and yet it wasn't.

From the cross Jesus was heard to say, "It is finished" – which, of course, was true and yet not everything was finished. Why? Because almost immediately the controversy started. Had he really died; where was the body;

had people actually seen him, spoken to him, touched him since he was buried?

And for more than two thousand years the evidence has been examined and re-examined; theories have been proposed and demolished, but the bottom line is that each of us who is open to the truth, can find the truth.

But will the truth be believed or, like that disputed goal in 1966 which both was and wasn't a goal, depending on your opinion, will the debate continue to rumble on?

For what we might call the World Cup of Religious Events, the evidence is freely available for all of us to examine; the testimonies of witnesses remain open to scrutiny. So, don't let doubt be the winner.

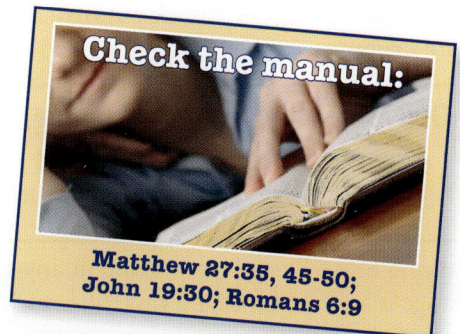

Check the manual:

Matthew 27:35, 45-50; John 19:30; Romans 6:9

When the dream is shattered

IT is not often a sporting celebrity is short of words but I can remember the occasion when a normally outspoken football star was (literally) speechless. The only response the interviewer got to his post-match questions was a slow shake of the head.

The occasion was a FA Cup semi-final which the player's side lost in the dying minutes of the game. Most sports-players and fans would agree that going out of a competition at that stage is among the worst of experiences. Knock-out matches are uncompromising, often cruel and

God ... witnessed, and through Jesus, his Son, experienced agony on every level

always tense. Being knocked out at any stage is a disappointment but the agony gets worse as you progress.

The tension builds, the stakes are higher, the pressure greater, the hopes and expectations pile on and then, for the fortunate few, you are just one step away from The Big One. OK, losing in a final is hardly great but at least you made it to the main attraction; you were there, enjoying the taste of something special; a rare moment of stardom to simply relish for its own sake.

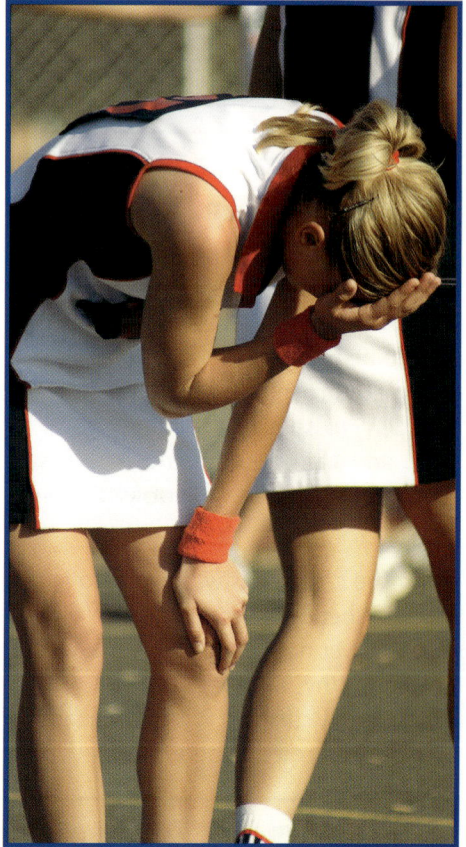

But who remembers the semi-final losers? A few, maybe, but honestly, not many. Which is why that player could not utter a single word. It was like falling at the final fence; the dream had been snatched away. It hurt and having to talk about it, and so soon after the disaster, hardly helped and probably added to the pain. Disappointment is one thing, but bitter, gut-wrenching disappointment is quite different. It carries with it an agony all of its own and unless you've been there, experienced it first-hand, you really don't know about it.

So would it surprise you to know God HAS been there, been to the lowest point imaginable. He witnessed, and through Jesus, his Son, experienced agony on every level – physical, emotional and spiritual. Jesus died and God allowed it.

Put like that it sounds shocking and in human terms it must have rated as a total failure; certainly his closest friends struggled to come to terms with it even though they had been forewarned. The fact that they had come so far, had achieved so much, just added to the pain and despair of the moment.

What Jesus did has left many a person speechless, not only because of what he did, but why he did it. He did it for us, each of us. It was the ultimate sacrifice, the ultimate act of selflessness. No, I can't explain it other than when we failed most, God succeeded most, and it has made all the difference for all eternity.

Check the manual:

**John 19: 28-30;
Romans 3: 23-26**

Do you understand?

OK, it's confession time. I was a football referee for twenty-two years and I have been umpiring cricket for about ten. As enjoyable and fulfilling as those activities have been, I still maintain that nothing beats actually playing the game.

Now, when I say officiating is enjoyable, and, in my experience, that has been so, most of the time, there are occasions when the edge can go off that enjoyment. For me that is most likely when players display their ignorance of the laws of the game they are playing!

Now I accept that in some games the laws or rules can be complex; some are open to a degree of interpretation and it is left to the official to rule by giving an opinion (fuelled by facts). That does add a tantalising element to our understanding of some decisions, even with modern technology and super-slow-mo television replays! Well, if nothing else, these minor controversies make for a lively debate over a beverage or two.

My gripe, however, is with the player who doesn't know or hasn't grasped the regulations under which he or she is

supposed to be playing. Surely, (and, yes, this is a cri de coeur), there is little excuse for not mugging up before taking to the field, on what is and is not permitted. Failing that, how I wish ignorance of the law were coupled with silence rather than complaint or dissent. End of gripe!

Well, not quite the end, as I now wonder if God isn't entitled to a gripe or two (or considerably more) when we

Compassion cannot be enforced because it is a matter of will

fail to differentiate right from wrong despite his laws being quite explicit. I am not referring solely to The Commandments because throughout the Bible we are presented with statements and examples of what God expects of us.

Indeed, in Jesus we have the perfect example of someone so in tune with and fulfilling God's expectations that,

by following him, we shouldn't go off-track. But Jesus' example is not merely one of obeying the rules. When we look more closely, we discover not only what he did but how he did it. And what we see is his compassion.

Laws can be enforced and they can be challenged. Compassion cannot be enforced because it is a matter of will. And neither can compassion be challenged, because compassion carries no desire for personal gain. That is Jesus' example; that is what he taught, that is what he demonstrated. Is that an example we can follow?

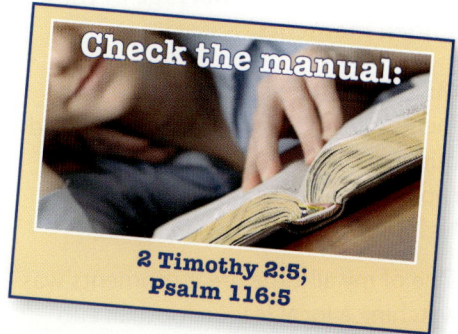

Check the manual:

2 Timothy 2:5;
Psalm 116:5

Who'd have thought it?

RECALLING sporting highlights is a very popular pastime. Most fans can rattle off a few good, if ever-so slightly embellished stories of magic moments when they witnessed something really special, maybe something unique. And, of course, with so much sport to play and watch, there is no shortage of these golden moments.

Mind you, some of the most memorable occasions were not played out at a major venue in front of a capacity crowd, nor did they feature high profile teams or individuals.

One of my all-time great moments was watching a local league football cup final. At the time I was chairman of a club that, prior to this particular season, had been somewhat undistinguished in its achievements. But this season was so different. Already league champions, 'the double' was within our grasp. One more big effort; and what an effort it proved to be.

After 90 minutes of heart-thumping drama with the advantage swinging one way, then the other, the score was 3-3. Extra time saw us nervously press forward as, with less than ten minutes to go, the deadlock remained unbroken.

And then we scored and shortly afterwards the coveted trophy was lifted. Unbelievable! You should have heard our supporters, all forty of them, go wild!

No, that piece of football history did not make the back pages of the tabloids; it hardly warranted a paragraph in the local newspaper, but those who played and those who watched were completely unfazed by the media's lack of interest.

Perhaps, rather like a birth or a death, they mean the world to those who were there, those who were close, but little

> ## ... a passing word may mean little at the time but who knows what that may become in the future?

to anyone else ... unless ... unless the event heralds something much bigger. Yes, I am now thinking of a birth in a stable and a death on a cross.

There would have been other births in other stables, given that stables were integral to most ordinary residences, and there were numerous executions by crucifixion. But as the significance of that one birth and death became

established, the magnitude of what had occurred was beyond measure.

On a much smaller scale it does remind us that the significance of a simple act or a passing word may mean little at the time, but who knows what that may become in the future? Sometimes, much later, we may discover that it was our action or our word that helped to transform a situation or even a life. We cannot know, and most times will probably never find out, but that is no reason to doubt the potential significance of the apparently insignificant.

Check the manual:

2 Corinthians 13:11;
1 Thessalonians 5:11

No pain; no gain?

IN high intensity, contact sports we take for granted the crunching impact, the sprawling bodies and the groans, grunts and gasps as breath is forced out of lungs. Most of the time the player(s) get up, exchange nods to confirm that most, if not all, bodily parts are still intact and functioning, and hasten off to rejoin the game.

But there are occasions, fortunately a rarity, when all is not well. Certainly at a professional level, players instinctively know if someone, be it colleague or

> **Watching someone suffer is never easy, especially if we are helpless to ease the pain**

opponent, has sustained something more than a temporary inconvenience as a result of taking a hit. Internal alarm bells ring; a sixth sense discerns that something is badly wrong and that this is not a sly attempt to gain an unfair advantage.

It is then that compassion and sympathy take over from competition. In sport we may be in opposition to one another but we are of the same spirit, we understand the thrills and also the risks and we also understand

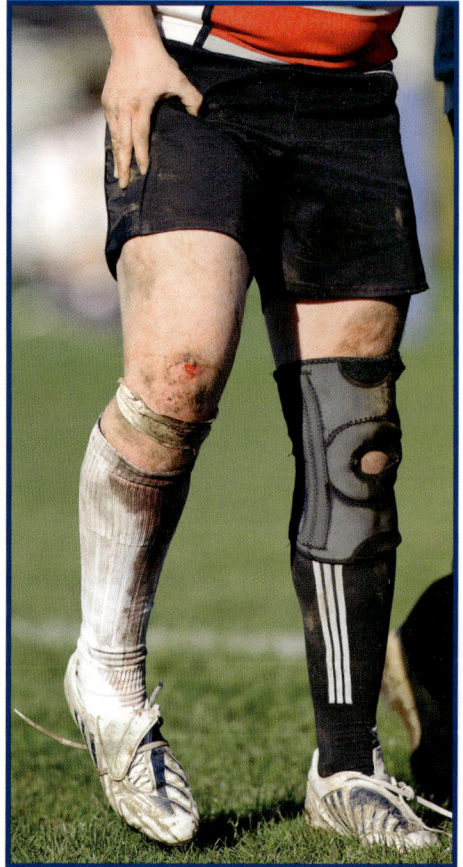

that an injury sustained by another player could have happened, indeed, one day may happen, to us.

Watching someone suffer is never easy, especially if we are helpless to ease the pain. I have seen big men wince and unashamedly wipe away tears while watching on helplessly as a fellow player is carried off. The fact is we all have a threshold both for experiencing pain and for witnessing it.

To read of Jesus that "He hung and suffered" is chilling. To know he hung and suffered for us is overwhelming and, at the same time, deeply disturbing. Why would anyone do that? It can only be down to a love and compassion beyond our comprehension, and that just about sums it up.

Is it so odd, then, that some are moved to tears or brought to their knees when they come to realise the generosity and the sacrifice that is expressed by the symbol of Christ suffering and dying for us?

Seeing another person suffer leaves its mark. It is hard, and for some impossible, to shake off the memory of having witnessed at close quarters someone suffer a severe injury. For those who come to a realisation that Christ suffered for us, it is as if an indelible mark is made on their lives. From that time on we are at one with him, bound together in the precious knowledge that the greatest good really did come from the greatest suffering.

Check the manual:

Luke 23:26-46;
Romans 8:35-39

Glory be!

SOME of the biggest names in sport have become so revered that the adulation and near-worship given to them by devout fans is just a bit beyond my understanding.

Those who have little, if any, interest in sport are bemused – not to say irritated – by the disproportionate attention given to someone whose primary achievement in life appears to centre on running or jumping or kicking or hitting. I daren't even approach the subject of the remuneration these stars receive for what I have heard called "trivial, inconsequential, self-indulgent activity". Ouch!

As sports fans we will see things differently but even we can wince when five figure sums are paid to professionals for a week's work. If we reframe what

There is a road to glory and on the way challenges have to be met ...

sportspeople do by placing it under the heading of entertainment, it may sit more easily on our consciences, though I know the harshest critics will still not be silenced.

Away from the world of the professionals, where the only effect on the participant's bank balance is a negative one, as kit is purchased and subscriptions paid, there does remain something for which there is no price tag: and that is glory. In my view there is nothing at all wrong with a bit of glory if it comes as a result of genuine achievement. Glory is a reward. It cannot be measured in a currency but it is a state that is recognised and valued.

Of course, others have opportunities to bask in glory that is not essentially theirs. Sports fans will have done very little themselves – apart from handing over their hard-earned cash at entrance gates and buying merchandise at grossly inflated prices – to help deliver success and the associated glory to those they support. But nothing is going to deny those fans a taste of glory when it comes their way.

Whether player or fan, a glimpse, let alone a taste of glory is not just handed over. There is a road to glory and on the way challenges and barriers have to be faced and overcome. Glory awaits the Christian at the end of his or her road; it is something that is assured. There is no denying the many demands on the way, but this glory is real, it is lasting and it is personal.

We know that for a sportsperson or a fan, glory will fade away. We talk of living past glories, especially when we are unlikely to reach such dizzy heights again. So to know that the glory we are promised will not fade must surely be, well, glorious!

Check the manual:

Romans 5:2; Colossians 1:27

PLANET SPORT

Top sportsmen and women are role models and fans hang on to their every word.

The Christian testimonies of top players can be highly effective. *2K plus* shares testimonies with sports fans to introduce them to Jesus.

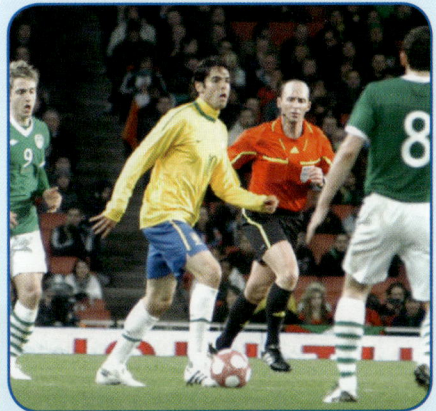

The Brazil midfielder Kaká was FIFA World Player of the Year in 2007. Two years later he left AC Milan to join Real Madrid after a fee of £59 million. Kaká is a committed follower of Jesus:

" *I was baptized at the age of 12. This was a very important step in my walk with Jesus. It makes me happy to read the Bible every day, to study it and to be in fellowship with God and learn more and more about Jesus.* "

The let-down and the pick-up

HE got sent off and we were down to ten men. She said she was fit but it soon became obvious she was not. He took a wrong turn when he should have known the route by heart.

Being let down by others, especially others you trust, can be an awful, gut-wrenching experience. You had thought your team-mate or your coach or whoever it is on whom you depend, was up to it, would deliver the goods, would be utterly reliable. But it all goes badly wrong; they make a mistake and your chance of success is blown. You don't want to blame, to point the finger but it is obviously their fault and yet you are the one to suffer. So are you bitter, resentful, angry? You have every reason to be, but then again, don't we all make mistakes, haven't we all fallen short of the ideal?

But they could have done better; it was their job and they failed; if they weren't

For God to offer forgiveness in spite of all we have done is quite amazing

up to it or didn't want to do it, why didn't they say so and get out before it really mattered? It feels like a betrayal

and in that position it may be hard to understand, let alone forgive.

Facing up to disappointment when we have done all that is required of us, but others have fallen short, is a bitter pill to swallow but to allow that feeling to fester is like allowing a poison slowly to work its way through our system. Ultimately, it is self-destructive.

On the surface the alternative seems just as unattractive. You cannot dismiss what has happened but you can come to terms with it within yourself and, most importantly, be reconciled with the one who has been responsible for the damage.

Am I talking about forgiveness? Well yes, in part, and forgiving can be a tough ask, but sometimes being forgiven is even tougher. When people have done wrong, and they know it, and they own up to it, they expect to suffer for their wrong-doing. To be told that

while it is not exactly 'OK' nonetheless they are forgiven, is deeply challenging.

As the guilty party, you expect to be left out, shunned, ignored, so to be received back, to be invited to rebuild relationships is not that easy; in fact it is asking a great deal of both parties.

For God to offer forgiveness in spite of all we have done is quite amazing. For us to humbly accept his forgiveness is not so much an end to matters as a new beginning, and with it all the challenges that can bring.

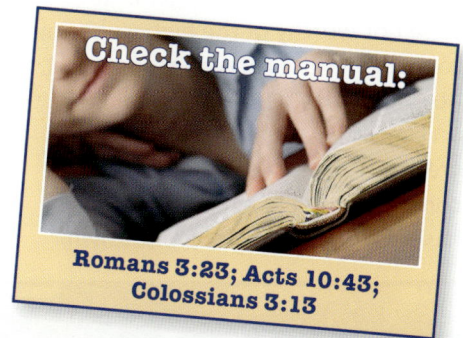

Check the manual:

Romans 3:23; Acts 10:43; Colossians 3:13

2K plus reports from major sports events such as ... The FIFA World Cup©.

In 2010 the FIFA World Cup came to Africa for the first time. Operating from the offices and studios of broadcast partners TWR in Johannesburg we produced match reports, interviews with fans at the Games, player testimonies and round table discussions in English and Spanish. Listeners to over 1500 radio stations heard our World Cup service in more than 30 countries.

www.2kplus.org.uk

Better – and better still

ONE of the more bizarre stories I have ever read concerned a lady who entered a cake-making contest and was awarded second prize. So what was so odd about that? She was the only contestant.

The judges decided that her efforts were not worthy of the highest honour so made her the runner-up to … well, no one! It may be true that being acclaimed first in a field of one is no great cause for celebration but, well, coming second in a field of one really has to be something of a put-down.

However, before we completely rubbish the field of one, I have watched the serious efforts of individuals pushing themselves to the limit without there

Achievements in sport – as in many aspects of life – are relative

being another soul in sight, and then seeing them being thrilled or deflated depending on the outcome. For them the best outcome is the genuine achievement of setting a new personal best performance.

Achievements in sport, as in many aspects of life, are relative. There is the local rugby team which had never won a match but when it did, for the first time, you would have thought the Heineken Cup was the prize. And there is the high jumper who had never made the cut to the second round but was beside herself with elation the day she progressed. I am full of admiration for the cyclist who, because of a chronic health condition has yet to complete a road race and yet at each outing manages to add a mile or so to the distance covered.

It is quite wrong to dismiss these achievements as anything less than praiseworthy, not least because they are the very essence of a right sporting mentality. For a few, winning is a habit; for most, reaching personal markers is evidence of progress and improvement and is rightly celebrated. While the medals and bouquets may continue to be handed over to the usual suspects, there is no denying the joy of the many other winners.

I know that at schools' sports days an everyone-a-winner philosophy prevails, and I can understand why, if nothing else it reduces the risk of tears and tantrums. But being determined to do well and then to do better, really is worth celebrating, irrespective of age.

For us all, the opportunities to improve, to reach up, out or over are before us on a daily basis, and not just in sport. Doing better, and then better still, in all we do can be applied to every facet of life. And if that improves the wellbeing of others through a well chosen or timely action or word, then our achievements will reflect far more than we can measure.

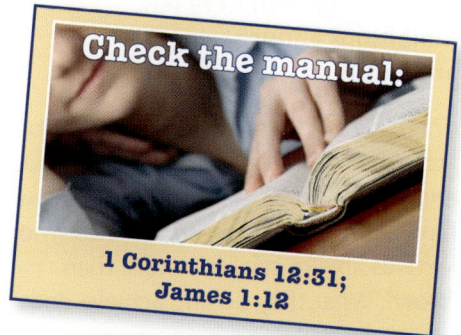

Check the manual:

1 Corinthians 12:31;
James 1:12

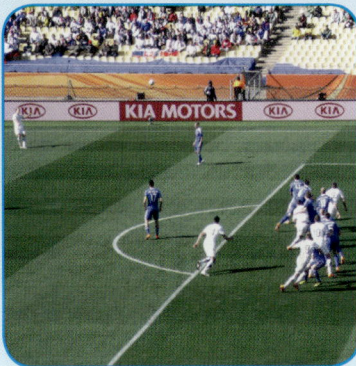

" We have been very impressed with the great *Up For The Corner!* programmes you have provided during the 2010 FIFA World Cup. It's been great to have a Christian view on the tournament and you guys really brought that across. Our listeners have very much enjoyed the show. " BRANCH FM, DEWSBURY.

Will you help us in this valuable ministry to radio listeners in the UK and around the world? Your donation will make a difference and, with your prayers, change lives.

www.2kplus.org.uk *(Please see page 64 for more details)*

I wonder

I have learned that children teach us more than we ever realise and, probably, more than we care to believe. Sometimes it is the quirkiness of their interpretations on life; sometimes it is their persistence in requiring answers to unanswerable questions. Perhaps the most telling aspect is their openness to awe and wonder. Children have few inhibitions about saying, "Wow", and meaning it.

There are plenty of good athletes whose achievements we acknowledge, applaud and enjoy watching. But there are a few, I might even say, very few, athletes who leave us able to say little more than "wow". What they do and achieve does

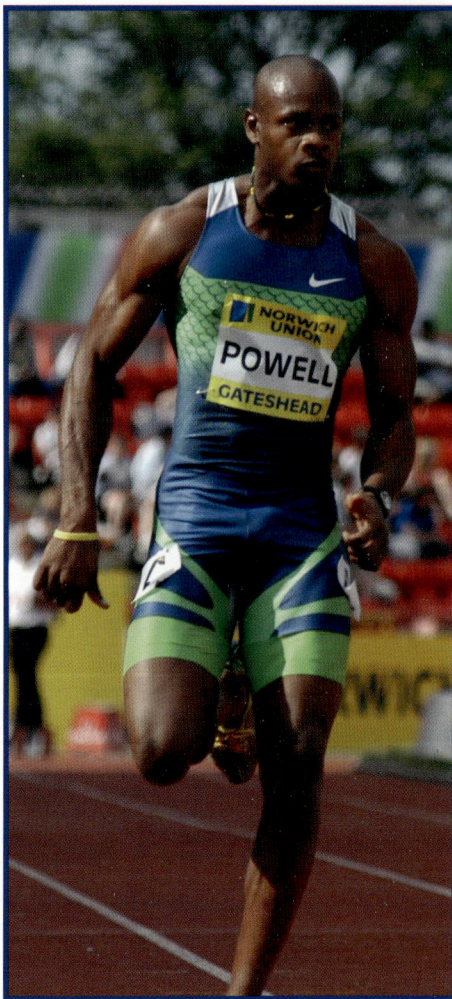

Jamaican sprinter Asafa Powell

... awe and wonder is evident in what God has given and in what God has done

far more than merely impress us; it leaves us stunned. It is jaw-droppingly amazing. We are genuinely in awe of them.

The first time I saw some top class gymnasts perform in competition, I was speechless. I was watching with someone who had himself taken part at quite a senior level but when I realised he, too, was just lost in wonder, I appreciated just how outstanding was this performance.

It is this sense of awe and wonder, almost childlike in terms of our response to something or someone, that lifts us out of the mundane and ordinary to a totally different plane. We even talk about being 'taken out of ourselves'. It is that combination of disbelief, admiration and just pure exhilaration that takes hold of us and leaves us in a state of near euphoria.

In a quite different context, we can watch TV programmes about space or medicine or nature and be at one and the same time informed and impressed. But if the presenter is a specialist in the subject and he or she conveys a sense of awe and wonder, then our experience is really elevated. We are no longer merely receiving interesting information; it is as if we are being drawn into a different dimension.

Unsurprisingly, awe and wonder are frequently associated with religious experiences, the most obvious ones being a meeting with God. These can be difficult to speak about as they are highly personal and, frankly, not so easy to describe in human terms. But, undoubtedly, awe and wonder is evident in what God has given and in what God has done.

So as you look around, as you discover and learn more of the world in which God has placed us, allow yourself a 'Wow' or two. And as you consider how God has worked in your life, add a few more 'Wows'. God really is awesome and wonderful.

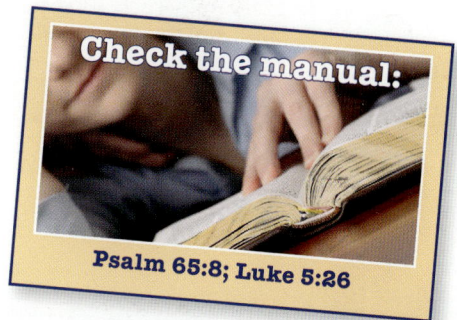

Check the manual:

Psalm 65:8; Luke 5:26

Devotional podcast resource

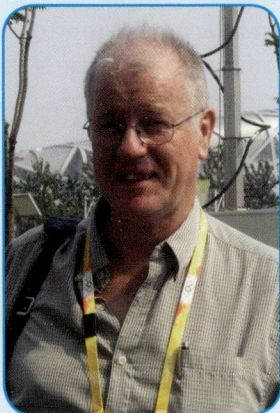

Have you ever wondered where you can find short audio devotionals exploring the relationship between sport and faith in Jesus Christ? You need look no further than our website!

Stuart Weir from partner group Verité Sport has produced four series which consider a Biblical perspective on sport to encourage the person who both loves sport and follows Jesus. *The Bible and Sport, Competition, 1 Peter* and *The Ten Commandments* are available free to download or listen to online at:

www.2kplus.org.uk

No place to go?

THE dreaded moment arrives. It happened every week and felt just as bad every time it happened. I am referring to the team-picking ritual humiliation that so many less than sporty-types had to endure at sports fields and in school playgrounds, and I expect it still happens, if now frowned upon in these enlightened times.

Two sides have to be selected and captains take turns to choose from the assembled ranks until the quota is reached. But, inevitably, some are left; some don't make the cut and, for them, hanging around watching others have a great time or, alternatively, drifting off for some lesser activity, are the unexciting options.

Oh to be one of the elite or even just one of the in crowd rather than the also-rans, or worse, the did-not-runs! Life is cruel; it can seem grossly unfair and, let's face it, discrimination of all kinds remains rife. We like to think that there is a place for everyone, and, of course, there is, but it isn't always where and with whom we would wish it to be.

So to find a place, indeed a gathering, where there are no restrictions, where a genuine welcome is assured and where what each of us has to offer is valued, sounds too good to be true. So where should we be looking for this most attractive of places and are there any conditions of entry?

Let's consider the last question first. Entry is free but by invitation though, interestingly, the invitation has already

Oh to be one of the elite or even just one of the in crowd rather than the also-rans ...

been issued; it merely awaits your acceptance. The invitation is to God's kingdom and Christ has issued it because his greatest desire is that we should enjoy participating in the greatest of gatherings, the gathering of God's people.

Yes, I know it's a bit overwhelming and may feel somewhat out of reach, not to mention beyond our comprehension. So for now, let's keep our feet on the ground and look more locally.

The church exists to prepare us for what God has in store, so it has a responsibility to reflect God's generosity and openness.

It may not always give the right impression and it can go about its task in a rather clumsy way but, if it is fulfilling its role as it should, it will receive us all, enabling us to catch a glimpse of and feel the touch of God's unconditional love and acceptance.

All can come in; no one need feel left out. The fellowship is genuine and participation is encouraged. There is no need to wander off; stay and take your place. Just one thing, please do accept the invitation.

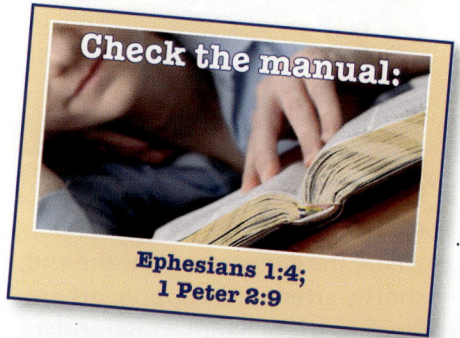

Check the manual:

Ephesians 1:4;
1 Peter 2:9

Thanks for what?

FORTUNATELY, in most sporting contests, however hard and gruelling the engagement, at the end, or shortly afterwards, opponents are content to shake hands, congratulate one another, offer consoling words and, in particular, to thank each other for the game.

Even the officials, despite the abuse they may have suffered during the match, will generally be acknowledged with some appreciative words for the part they played. After all the tension and energy have dissipated, are these words just a part of the post-encounter ritual, the 'done thing', or is there more to it?

I was watching a rugby match in a local park and got chatting to a player who had been substituted during the second half. He had had a good game but, as they say, "the tank was now empty!" He was satisfied with his performance and not unhappy for the chance to sit out the rest of the match.

Puffing and panting, somewhat, he admitted, "I am just thankful to still be playing". He then explained how he had suffered a serious accident at work and with the added concern of complications after surgery was advised that his mobility might be severely limited, permanently.

He described his difficulty in coming to terms with this; how, for him, as an active, sociable, young man, it was devastating as he visualised being deprived of a major part of his life.

Many people have a deep desire to have their lives changed

Without emotion or exaggeration he then told me about the support he had received, from physiotherapists, family and friends who motivated and enabled him to recover sufficiently to re-engage with his passion for sport.

As he finished unlacing his boots and headed off to the changing rooms, he added, "I cannot thank them enough for changing my life around; I give thanks every day."

Many people have a deep desire to have their lives changed but the changes they seek are not necessarily visible to the wider world. A change of heart, a change of outlook on life, (and death, for that matter); a change in how they treat others; just some of the inner changes that may seem out of reach.

Some changes can take a lifetime to complete but taking the first steps towards change will at least get the process underway. The Bible encourages us to be different and to become different we have to be prepared to make changes. And as each change is achieved, there is something for which to be thankful. Thank God, who makes the difference.

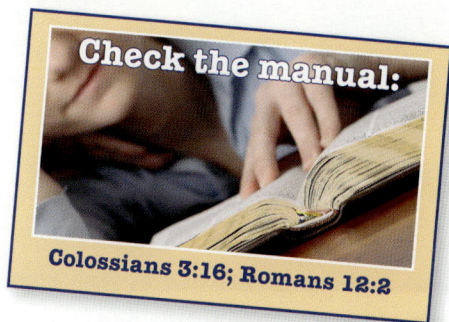

Check the manual:

Colossians 3:16; Romans 12:2

2K plus **reports from major sports events such as ...
The ICC Cricket World Cup.**

Former Zimbabwe cricketer Henry Olonga (left) provided comment and analysis for radio listeners during the 2011 World Cup with a Christian perspective. Zimbabwe spin bowler Ray Price talked about his cricket career and faith in Jesus; we also produced testimonies of former players including Suruj Ragoonath (West Indies) and Shaun Pollock (South Africa):

"I look back on my career and know that God has blessed me and that everything I've achieved is thanks to him."

Glorious anticipation

OUR bus had made the 250-mile journey in very good time and so there were still two hours before the match was due to start. Fans from the two teams were wandering about and there were plenty of good humoured exchanges as we passed one another.

Taking the opportunity for some light refreshment, a few of us got into conversation with a small group of the opposition's supporters. After one or two inevitably provocative comments we actually embarked upon a series of enthralling discussions about the strengths and weakness of the sides, past glories (and some embarrassing failures), along with some general chat.

As time passed we became more focussed on the imminent event and we heard ourselves trying to anticipate special moments; the likelihood of star players putting in a stunning, match-winning display; envisaging the trophy being lifted aloft; generally anticipating the glorious moments that we hoped would fuel a memorable experience.

How, then, might we have felt if the glorious moments we were anticipating looked for all the world like disastrous moments? Jesus' friends listened as he spelt out the glorious moments he was anticipating. But they came across as moments of highly-charged confrontation, of unjust arrest, of torture and execution. And yet, somehow all this was being presented as a means to glory. It didn't seem to make sense.

Up to that point most things had made sense. People who were ill, were healed; people without hope, found hope;

The road to glory has to be anticipated in its entirety

people who had no one to believe in, believed in Jesus. Surely these things were closer to being glorious than a series of gruesome experiences that ended with death on a cross.

But there is something missing here. The road to glory has to be anticipated in its entirety. Death was not the end. Death led to resurrection – and, as such, victory over the one thing that no person other than Jesus could overcome. And, because of that victory, we can have a glorious anticipation of both life with Jesus now and, beyond death, a resurrected life continuing with him.

OK, it is a hard thing to get our minds around and, rather like my anticipating what would happen in the match yet to be played, our anticipation of what will happen as life unfolds now, let alone later, is not going to be entirely clear. Frankly, we don't know about it in anything other than general terms. But this I am sure about: it will be glorious.

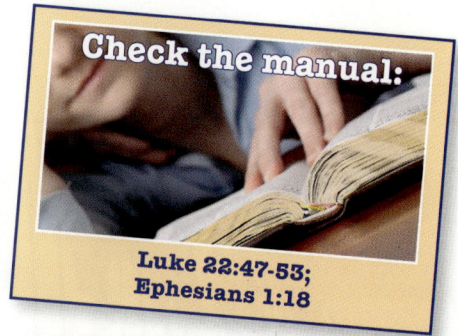

Check the manual:

Luke 22:47-53;
Ephesians 1:18

Looking for inspiration?

AT international sporting events there are usually those poignant moments before the contest begins when flags are raised and national anthems are sung.

There is little doubt that players and fans alike feel inspired by the lifting up of flags and voices and, if nothing else, this curtain-raise provides a dramatic prelude to the anticipated encounter. But away from the big stage of such events, from where do you draw inspiration?

I tend to look back at those I have met over the years who offered me a sense of what was possible and achievable in life. I think particularly of those from modest backgrounds, those who could boast of neither wealth nor position to ease their way in life. But what they did have was vision, conviction, commitment and resolve.

One person I worked for said he was looking for colleagues more prepared to say "why not?" than "why?" His philosophy was to try things out, to take (calculated) risks and then to be ready to be surprised, and hopefully delighted, by what happened.

But there are, for a follower of Jesus, other sources of inspiration. We can be inspired by the Word of God, by which I mean both its message and the messengers. There are many extraordinary characters to be found in the pages of the Bible but there are also many ordinary characters to be found there. But what makes this so inspirational is to see how the ordinary was transformed into the extraordinary.

By the time Jesus comes on the scene, the variety of characters, their backgrounds, their problems, their hopes, seem to cover every type of human condition. The common feature was their being inspired by the man who transformed their lives. None was the same again.

Some people who are inspirational can seem remote, distant figures. We may be inspired by them but can never see ourselves aspiring to what they are or what they have achieved. It is quite the opposite with Jesus. He makes himself accessible. He actually invites us to come and follow and the closer we allow ourselves to get to him, the more we will know him and the more we will be inspired to be like him.

But now a question; could you inspire others? I am not suggesting that we set ourselves up as inspirational figures, but the more we are able to show others what we have found to be inspirational in Jesus, the more others will be inspired to be like him. So my question becomes: could you become a channel for Jesus to inspire others?

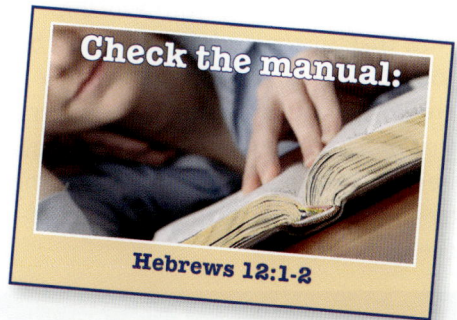

Check the manual:

Hebrews 12:1-2

Trying to be humble

YOU have to admit that some of our sporting stars really know how to work a crowd. When you are that good at what you do, the fans are going to go pretty wild when you deliver the goods. It has now become part of the act to get a reaction from the spectators.

Of course it is just that, an act. It is all part of the fun, all part of the show, urging the crowd to appreciate you, to cheer you, to worship you? Worship? Now that, surely, is adulation gone a bit too far! After all, worship implies you are worthy and is anyone really worth that much, however talented they may be? Maybe I'll leave that question in the air and take a look at the other end of the spectrum.

What about humility? "No, no, it was nothing. I just tried my best and, on the day, I am pleased to say it all came together." Is that what we like to hear from our high achievers, the suggestion that they are not really so good and

In the bigger scheme of things there is plenty about which we should be humble

therefore, maybe, we shouldn't make a fuss of them? How unfair, how ungracious. We want to make a fuss of them and we want them to respond as if we are right to make a fuss of them.

Or there are those who deflect all the praise towards others. "I couldn't have done any of it without the support of

my family/coach/colleagues/cat ..." Ok, perhaps not the cat. That, as a response, doesn't seem very satisfactory, either. After all, praise is a gift and when any gift is offered it is actually bad manners to have it rejected. If the praise is legitimate, it should be accepted; if it is praise that should be shared then acknowledge it and share it, but don't just bounce it on to someone else.

In the bigger scheme of things there is plenty about which we should be humble. That God should bless us in so many ways, that he should invite us to share the glory of his Kingdom through the gift of his Son, our Saviour. Well that is quite a lot to trigger some humility in anyone. And equally there is plenty of cause to worship God, who truly is worthy of our worship.

No, humility is not straightforward. If it appears false or contrived or lacks sincerity, it is a mockery of something that is an important strand in our witness as followers of Jesus. Be humble before God, certainly. Be humble in serving one another, but be genuine in receiving praise and appreciation, and be genuine and generous in offering praise and in appreciating others.

Check the manual:
Proverbs 22:4; 1 Peter 5:5

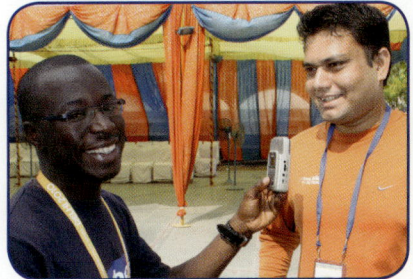

Fair enough

WELL done; good game; you beat me fair and square. That's the way it goes sometimes. I enjoy playing but I also enjoy winning, and faced with an opponent who is better than me or who has caught me on an off-day, I can't complain. In defeat, I have to grin and bear it, or grimace and bear it, and hope I can do better next time, or hope my opponent has an off-day!

What is harder, much harder to bear is when I have been beaten – but not fair and square. There will be occasions when I know, or suspect, that someone is bending the rules, or doing something underhand to give them that winning edge.

Sometimes it is down to the officials to spot what has happened and to take appropriate action, but what about when we are playing a friendly game on trust, the trust being that our opponent(s) will keep to the rules and not take an unfair advantage? We actually talk about "playing the game" meaning we expect honesty.

I reckon most true sports fans are pretty fair-minded. They want to see their side

or hero win but they also want to see a good contest. Delivering the winner you want but with little entertainment value is not really satisfying. In fact true fans can feel short-changed despite having a win to celebrate.

The same fair-minded fans will be uneasy when a win has come through deceit or deception, by conning or

Of course, some cheats do prosper – but there is a cost

fraud. Of course, some cheats do prosper – but there is a cost. Fans value reputation and a reputation is soon tarnished when the player shows him/herself not to be the true article.

Exceptional skill and talent are rare enough commodities and that is what attracts us to watch and support those who are so gifted. When those gifts are devalued by deliberately seeking to gain an unfair advantage, fans are not fooled and while they tolerate or overlook an occasional lapse, patience can wear thin.

None of us is perfect; we all make mistakes. Often they will be by accident and we will regret them and try to make amends. But sometimes our mistakes arise from errors of judgment and such lapses will also cause us considerable regret.

Acknowledging what has been wrong is important – demanding, quite possibly, but important. Those we have wronged need to know of our regret and our desire to do something about it. And God needs to know of our regret – because he desires to forgive us and restore us and to continue to fashion each of us into the person he wants us to be.

Check the manual:

Psalm 33:5;
Colossians 3:13

Achieving excellence

BRILLIANT, fantastic, genius, stunning. The superlatives flow as we watch, admire, yes, and probably envy the achievements of the sporting elite. We know excellence when we see it and we may even covet it.

Actually, as coveting goes, it is not such a bad thing in this context. The Bible says that "if anything is excellent or praiseworthy – think about such things." And more than that, "eagerly desire the greater gifts. And I will show you the most excellent way."

Now try turning this on its head. What is not excellent in your life? To which my answer would be: "How long have you got?"

Achieving excellence is impossible without ... a passion for excellence

The list is embarrassingly long and I am not about to share it with anyone! OK, that is how life is for most of us; somewhat less than excellent. But the crucial question is: "Do you want to achieve excellence?" Yes, I'm up for that – who wouldn't be? But how to achieve it; that's a big question.

Let's be realistic; this is a one-step-at-a-time project. True, there are those whose lives have been dramatically

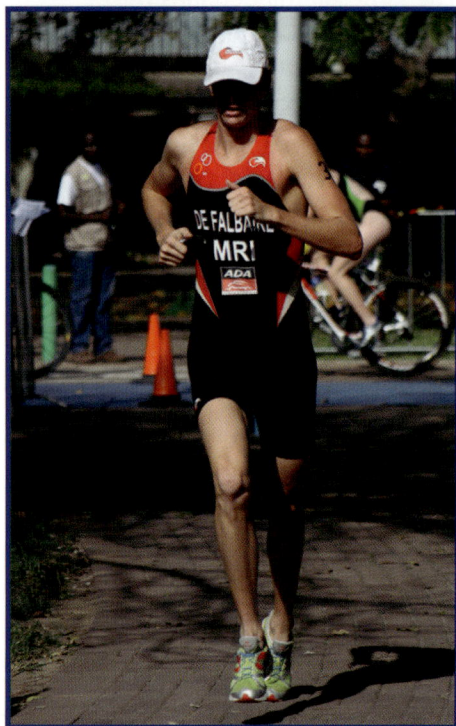

turned around and for them, for now, everything is wonderful. But I'm focussing on those of us who have to graft at being different, at gradually becoming excellent.

So, here is a way to make a start. Prepare a list, and make it a short one, of a few less-than-outstanding aspects of your everyday life. These are things that fall short of the ideal you would hope to attain. Alongside each, note one change that would improve the situation. Already too daunting? Then think small and think achievable. Remember, Olympic pole vaulters didn't start by leaping over double-decker buses.

So you now have a few tasks and are working towards improving your performance. Keep those tasks in mind over a week or so and then take stock of your progress. What have you learned; what you have attained?

You may learn that some areas present you with a tougher challenge than you had expected while others were easily addressed. Remind yourself of the incentive of becoming like Christ as a way to keep you on task.

Achieving excellence is impossible without a desire – no, more than just a desire, a passion for excellence. The mindset must be: Good enough is NOT good enough. So start expecting to do better and, as you build upon the original list, expect also to grow in confidence that you can bring about change.

Hold before you the image of Christ because he wants you to be like him; a child of God becoming an excellent child of God.

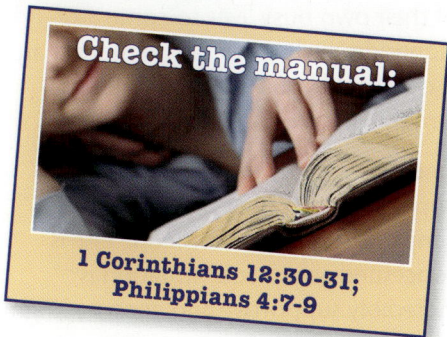

Check the manual:

1 Corinthians 12:30-31;
Philippians 4:7-9

Now that's encouraging

WHEN a team goes five matches without winning or when a player continues to underachieve, even the most dedicated fan starts to ask a few questions.

In my experience fans are remarkably tolerant, philosophical, positive and accepting of the dips in performance, though, of course, there will always be some who immediately call for heads to roll.

The majority, however, seem ready to accept the bad times along with the good times, to ride out what they

We have to be prepared to face all the experiences that come our way

would label a temporary loss of form and look ahead to the improvement they feel sure will happen. The call most often heard is to "hang in there" and wait for a turnaround in fortunes, which will come.

When times are tough and success is fading into a distant memory, some fans send messages of support to players or the coaches. You might call these "a word in season". Many of us have had something similar happen when we are

down for whatever reason. The unexpected call, the timely email or text, even a handwritten card or letter; examples of someone taking time out of their own busy lives to come alongside, perhaps to say no more than "I care" or "I know it's miserable" or "anything I can do?"

Finding the right words really is less important than offering some words. Simply to know that someone else is concerned about your situation is incredibly supportive and encouraging.

As followers of Jesus we have not been promised detours to avoid life's disappointments, sorrows, frustrations or failures. We have to be prepared to face all the experiences that come our way, and to be grateful to and for those who come alongside in our times of need.

But equally, we have a responsibility to encourage and support those we meet who are struggling. In so doing we are not to differentiate nor discriminate between either individuals or needs, but rather we are to help in turning things around.

All this may sound like nothing more than being a good neighbour, and in a sense that is exactly what it is. But we can bring rather more to these situations. We can bring the love of Christ; we can bring his presence and his peace. In this, our actions may well speak far louder than any words.

And here is a lesson we can learn from sports fans. They rate loyalty very highly. It is a mark of true fans that they are not easily won over by others. They do not switch camps on a whim. Many testify to their allegiance being lifelong. Maybe that can serve to remind us all to take our God-given responsibilities seriously.

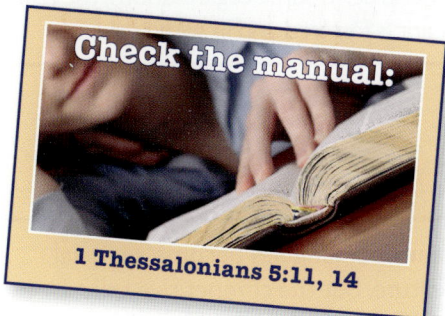

Check the manual:

1 Thessalonians 5:11, 14

2K plus
INTERNATIONAL SPORTS MEDIA

2K plus reports in several languages at major sports events. Pedro Arias is our Spanish producer.

Pedro reports for sports fans listening to radio stations in South America, Europe and worldwide on the internet. During the 2010 FIFA World Cup about 1000 radio stations broadcast Pedro's reports, features and interviews with a Christian perspective.

Radio Familia 96.9FM in Cuenca, Ecuador was one of the stations that broadcast Pedro's reports from the 2008 Olympic Games in Beijing:

"You were a real blessing. Our station has programming based on Christian principles aiming at a non-Christian audience. Having these sports reports captivated our audience and contributed to our production."

www.2kplus.org.uk

Taking one for the team

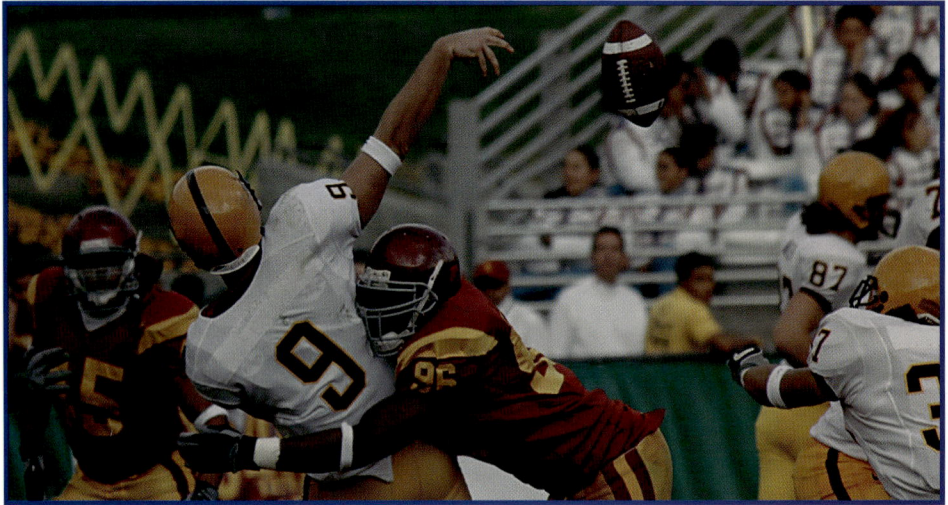

I T was while watching a game of American Football that I first heard the phrase. Unable to see a clear path to pass the ball, the quarterback clung on while allowing himself to become buried under a mountain of bodies. As the opposing team peeled themselves off the groaning heap, the last man to get up, didn't.

A little later, as he was helped from the field to be greeted as a hero, the coach was full of praise for him 'taking one for the team'. I didn't hear the player's response, but probably the excruciating pain limited his desire and ability to speak.

In sport there can be opportunities for such a sacrificial gesture which, while possibly reckless in itself, nonetheless benefits the team as a whole. But what about in other aspects of life? To what extent do we put ourselves out for each other?

We have probably come to accept that life can be very competitive; it's me against the rest and I have to look after number one. True, in some organisations, the team spirit is fostered and in some cases

To suffer in the place of another is as amazing as it is rare

team-building has become a crucial feature, but the competitive spirit is never far below the surface. In a team we may be equals, but who is going to emerge as first among equals?

An ancient prayer contains the telling line, "To give and not to count the cost" which says a great deal about both priority and attitude. It reflects a plea to be able to put others first and to do so with an attitude of selflessness.

Love can be expressed in no greater way than in being willing to lay down one's life for another. To suffer in the place of another is as amazing as it is rare. We probably hope we will never be put to the test for fear that we would fail, and yet Jesus suffered and died for us, and did so in place of us.

It is difficult to find the words to express what this means when we try to take it on board. The hymn writer, John Newton, coined the phrase "amazing grace" summing up all Jesus had done in his life and even today many people still find singing those words deeply moving.

In modern speak, Jesus' sacrifice was the ultimate in taking one for the team, when the team includes all people, in every age. How sad that so few of them acknowledge what he has done for them. We really ought to let them know.

Check the manual:

John 15:13; Hebrews 10:10

Capturing the moment

I had only a matter of seconds to get in position, point the camera and get what, for me, would be the shot of a lifetime. My hero appeared, walked towards me, looked in my direction at just the right moment and, albeit with finger trembling, I managed to press the button at just the right moment.

From time to time, even though it is now many years on, I glance back at the picture I took and allow myself a

Christine Ohuruogu, Great Britain's 400m 2008 Olympic champion

"Do you remember this?" my friend asked

satisfied smile as I recall how I captured the moment. That picture speaks volumes to me. It brings back such vivid memories of the player, the match, the whole day in fact. Brilliant!

Years after that, I was present at a quite different event when a friend with whom I had lost contact, met up with me. We were both attending a conference and as we were chatting he reached into his pocket and took out a picture. It was of an informal setting with people milling around and chatting. "Do you remember this?" my friend asked. I replied that I had only a vague memory. "It was at that event that my life was changed," he explained.

Then, as he described the situation, I realised that he was referring to the evening when he came to accept Jesus into his life. He went on to describe how he always carried the picture with him and that when he was really up against things and hard pressed, he would take out the picture which, for him, captured a life-transforming moment.

As he admitted, the picture itself would mean nothing to anyone else, but to him it would always be associated with a pivotal moment in his life as well as a prompt to thank God for that moment. The picture reminded him that God, who changed his whole life, was still God in his life.

For some people, faith develops over a period of exploring and discovering; for others it all seems to come together quite quickly. But there is always a story to be told. That story is about a life-change and it is the most significant story within a life. Capturing and holding the story so we can share it with others enables the power of God we have experienced to be presented to others.

It is not a case of a story being dramatic or sensational, merely being authentic. Such stories are unique because their focus is on that precious time when God engages with one he loves. It cannot be copied or borrowed. It is all yours, but so is the privilege to share it.

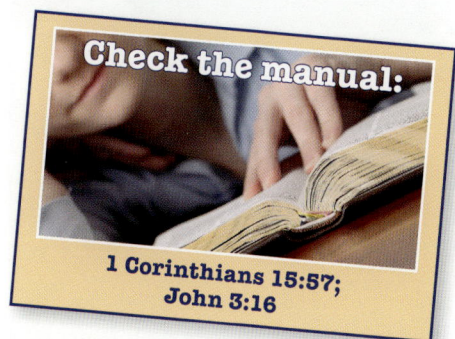

Check the manual:

1 Corinthians 15:57;
John 3:16

So close, and yet ...

SHE leapt high into the air, bent over and around the bar and cleared it, almost. She had fallen foul of the curse of the high jumper; the trailing foot, or rather the millimetre of shoe which just grazed the bar, just enough to nudge it off its perch.

With both grace and power he stroked the ball and watched it fly off the bat as everyone followed its progress, convinced they were seeing the perfect shot to win the match. But the ball stopped millimetres from the boundary line and the team were denied the winning run.

From an impossible angle the player launched the basketball towards the ring only to see it tantalisingly hover on the rim before falling the wrong side of the net.

So near and yet so far. So close and yet with nothing to show for the effort. You can replay these instances a thousand times in your head but the outcome remains unchanged. It just didn't turn out the way it might have.

These days we are used to seeing replays, at normal speed, slow motion, super-slomo, from multiple angles, all allowing commentators and pundits to

analyse minutely what happened, and even what didn't happen. And yet, still the bar falls, the ball stops short and no basket is scored.

Well, what did you expect? You can replay past events, but you cannot change them. What is done is done.

So what do we, as sports fans, expect to happen? We expect the athletes and the players to get on with it! We expect them to persevere. Certainly there are

You can replay past events, but you cannot change them

disappointments and setbacks; as fans we know all about them, but they are history. There may be some regrets but having taken note of what happened and learning from it, what will really make a difference next time?

Well, there may be all sorts of things to modify, adjust or practise but above all there will need to be a

determination to persevere. It is an important quality that marks out some sportspeople and it can mark us out too.

God knows us too well to expect us to get things right all the time, let alone first time. But he does expect us to acknowledge our shortcomings, to learn from them and then press on, persevere, because there is a target to aim for and a goal to be achieved in the life of a Christian. And, no, we are not there yet – but we can be closer, and get ever closer until … we will make it.

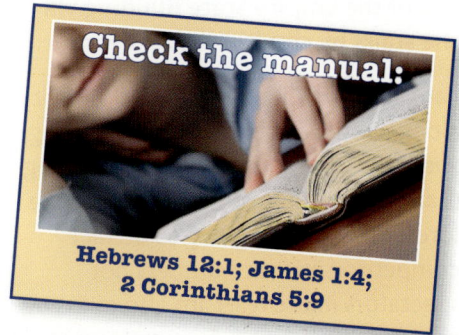

Check the manual:

Hebrews 12:1; James 1:4; 2 Corinthians 5:9

There must be another way!

ALICE McNamara is a champion. She completed the demanding course in the remarkably fast time of 13 minutes and 3 seconds, and, having reached the finishing line, she took a break to enjoy the panoramic view of New York. Her achievement? Winning the 2011 women's race to reach the top of the Empire State Building via the stairs by climbing 1576 steps.

I am guessing that this sporting activity, along with the likes of extreme ironing, stinging nettle eating and wife carrying (I am not kidding you!), are not, in the foreseeable future, going to attract competitors in vast numbers nor spectators in droves. I am also guessing

People find all sorts of ways to get themselves into the record books

that they are not on the list of sports waiting to be considered for inclusion in a future Olympics. Yet, in their own way, they are testimony both to that human quality for inventiveness and to our delight in the obscure and bizarre.

People find all sorts of ways to get themselves into the record books. In the process some also have their "15 minutes of fame" but then most people,

having heard the story of some novel achievement soon forget about it – though probably not before musing that there have to be other ways of making it to the sports headlines!

In fact the ways to a lasting achievement in sport, as in other spheres of life, are rather fewer than we may at first think. We may be able to recall the names and a few details of sporting stars from an era; we may be able to bring to mind a selection of celebrities that caught our attention but, for the most part, fame and status are fleeting, and those who attain them would be well advised to enjoy them while they last. All too soon, the golden moment will pass.

By contrast, the follower of Jesus is offered a prize and a status that lasts for ever. God's plan for us is less concerned with fleeting experiences than with eternal life. All that we experience now is but a step on the way to something that will last for ever. Of course, what we experience has a value in the bigger scheme of things; God is not asking us to make a quantum leap from here to eternity. In fact he wants us to taste eternity. Here. Now.

Can I describe it or explain it? Not very well, I'm afraid. That's the problem with the eternal and the everlasting; there's not a lot with which to compare it. But I'm content to know that it is from God and so it is good – in fact, very good. Taste and see; I think you'll agree.

Check the manual:

Philippians 3:14;
Romans 6:22

Hang in there

DURING twenty-two years as a football referee I had more than a few interesting moments. Looking back I have many cherished memories; memories such as my whistle-blowing visits to major venues, sharing the same turf as household names of the day.

But, as is the way of things for a referee, I started and ended my career in the more humble setting of the public park pitches. But it was here that I witnessed some equally memorable moments, not a few of them odd or even bizarre.

Among those that stand out was the occasion, in early January, when I was assigned to oversee a pretty inconsequential meeting between a university team and a local village side. It was a bitterly cold Saturday afternoon and, even before half time, I was not alone in wishing the minutes away. But then we had a bit of excitement, swiftly followed by a great deal of hysterical laughter.

The village team's striker shot at goal with surprising power and accuracy, forcing the university's six-foot-six keeper to leap up and tip the ball over the bar. Great shot; great save. And the game would have continued if it hadn't been for one thing. The keeper had jumped up but he hadn't come down. We looked, we stared, and then we fell apart.

The poor guy had become an innocent victim of a loving gift. As a Christmas gift, his girlfriend had knitted him an

... we had a bit of excitement, swiftly followed by a great deal of hysterical laughter

exceedingly chunky sweater and, it being so cold, he had chosen to wear it over his shirt. (A decision that may have been influenced by the presence of the current love-of-his-life at the match!)

At the crucial moment, as he nudged the ball to safety, his sweater became attached to one of the hooks supporting the goal net. Up he went and up he stayed; left dangling in mid-air. But, eventually, what goes up, has to come down, and so did he, bringing the

crossbar with him. Precious moments, trivial as they certainly are, are not lost. We recall and treasure them.

The gospel accounts are packed with precious moments from the life of Jesus. And it doesn't end there. Followers of Jesus, years after his death and resurrection, presented us with still more precious moments, moments of wonder, of admiration, of inspiration as the impact of Jesus expanded.

These are truly moments to recall and treasure, and there is nothing at all trivial about them. Open the pages and be touched by accounts that are so precious and yet so accessible. Hang on to the words, and be delighted.

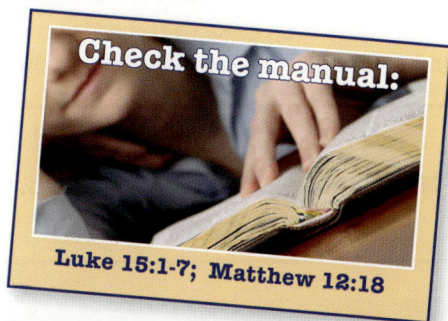

Check the manual:

Luke 15:1-7; Matthew 12:18

Crowd control

SO which are the most enthusiastic and passionate fans? Those who follow a Premier League club? Those whose team reach the Super Bowl? Formula One fanatics turning out in appalling weather to catch a glimpse of their heroes through the mist and spray? Or maybe the Barmy Army circling the globe to keep pace with the national side?

All good shouts but I don't think any of them come even close to the passion and fanaticism of a six-year-old's mother

> **I am more likely to respond to someone cheering me on … getting alongside me …**

at the annual school sports day. Believe me, I've been there and, reckless fool that I am, as a judge, and I have scars to prove it! If ever there was a case for photo-finish technology or stewards' enquiries, the playing field behind the classroom block is where the need is greatest.

Given that half the competitors are unaware of the rules of running, such as keeping to lanes, and some mothers lose all inhibitions (not to mention basic good manners and a civil tongue), the recipe for disaster, tears and

tantrums is ready-made. Not that the youngsters care a hoot, as long as the promised chocolate bar is delivered at the end of their ordeal.

Mind you, there are times in our lives when we really could do with similar, overwhelming support and encourage-ment aimed in our direction. There are darker days, perhaps a string of them, maybe even with no end to them in sight; when we feel isolated, victimised, unjustly dealt with and far from the blessed state we thought was ours as men and women who follow Jesus.

I suppose I should now be suggesting a response which requires dropping to our knees and embarking upon some earnest prayer. Sounds good but, frankly, sometimes it is just not that easy. But I am more likely to respond to someone cheering me on, urging me, getting alongside me, genuinely encouraging me.

It is certainly something we can do for others, but who is going to do it for us? Well, I've got some good news on that score because the Bible tells us there is a "cloud of witnesses" doing just that. It is a heaven-sent gift to us all; knowing that somewhere, somehow, "saints" are right with us. No one can run a race for us but as sure as a six-year-old's mother will give it everything to see her child through, so there are those who are unswervingly for us.

The Church's membership is not determined by a headcount of those currently attending worship on Sundays. Its membership is derived from all nations in every age. We represent but a fragment in a moment of its remarkable history. You would be right to be amazed at the support you have.

Check the manual:

Hebrews 12:1; Galatians 3:28

" Sport has the power to change the world, the power to inspire, the power to unite people in a way little else can. It speaks to people in a language they can understand. "

NELSON MANDELA

2K plus programmes and features are heard by listeners in parts of the world where it is not easy to be a follower of Jesus.

" I liked the segment regarding the Olympic Games. It is a marvellous programme. "

LISTENER IN PAKISTAN

" I found many interesting stories in your programme, especially *More Than Gold, Olympic Spirit*. It shows not only God's perfection but that God has created us in perfection. "

LISTENER IN CENTRAL ASIA

Please consider making a gift to help sports fans around the world discover Jesus and become his followers. Your donation will make a difference and, with your prayers, change lives.

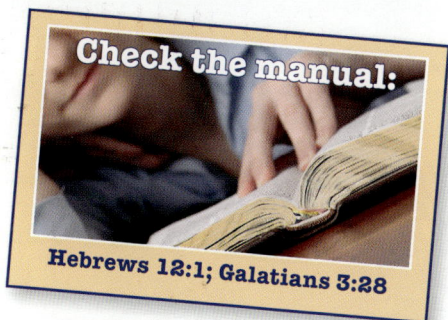

PLANET SPORT

Reporting from sports events across the globe

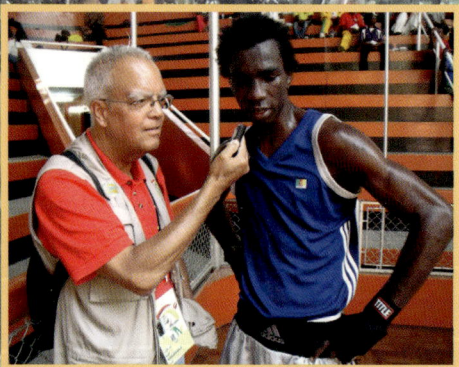